George Appleton

# ONE MAN'S PRAYERS

*Second Edition*

London
**SPCK**

D0967113

First published in 1967
Second edition 1977
Second impression 1977

SPCK
Holy Trinity Church
Marylebone Road
London NW1 4DU

Printed in Great Britain by
Bocardo & Church Army Press Ltd
Cowley, Oxford

ISBN 0 281 03573 3

# Contents

# Preface to the Second Edition

Most of these prayers came out of experience,
in situations in which I found myself, in
struggles for faith, sometimes in travail of
spirit, occasionally in moments of deep
communion with God. They were written
down, not primarily for publication, but
as recording a new insight to tranquillize,
guide, and strengthen my own spirit. They
came out of meditation and sometimes
from the still, quiet, intuiting prayer which
we call contemplation. I pray them now, to
re-awaken the soul and be led into Spirit-
guided thought and trusting stillness.

I am grateful to learn that they have helped
others, so that a further reprint seems
needed. I am equally grateful to SPCK for
being ready in a time of inflation to bring
out a completely new edition, re-set in short
lines which focus the attention on each
clause. In this way each prayer becomes a
meditation of mind and heart and lets the
wind of the Spirit carry the praying one into
his or her own communion with God.

The longer I meet people of other faiths
the more quietly confident I am that God
is at work among them as well as among
Christians. They have treasures of spiritual
experience to share with us, just as we share
with them the inexhaustible riches which we

are continually discerning in God's revealing and saving action in Christ Jesus. This is not to ignore the need of enlarged faith, deepening conversion, growing love to God and our fellow humans, and above all a more faithful embodiment of what we have already received.

The evidence of God at work in varying degrees in all religions, together with the widespread desire of people for a deeper spiritual life, leads me to believe that a new Pentecost is near, when God's outpouring of his spirit on all flesh will be realised and received more widely, deeply, gratefully, and transfiguringly.

✠ GEORGE APPLETON
   *August 1976*

# Prayers

These prayers were written over a period of ten years, primarily for my own use. Few of them have been prayed with other people. Some of them came almost spontaneously, without any conscious intention or effort. Others took a long time to word, rather like some of the inner groanings which St Paul mentions as being so difficult to express. Number 27, for example, was written and prayed during the weekend of the Suez crisis.

Others have definite associations. Number 28 was written after visiting the Gethsemane chapel in Coventry Cathedral. Numbers 29-32 are translations from the French, culled from several books on the Holy Spirit, which with some effort I read while staying with some good ecumenical friends in France. Others were written at the stimulation of H. A. Williams's essay in *Soundings*, and Number 46 owes much to Bishop John Robinson. Number 55 was written for Father Joe Williamson's work in East London.

A good number of prayers spring from my touch with people of other faiths; a further group spring from my growing knowledge of world hunger and world needs. Students of Teilhard de Chardin will recognize the help that he has been to my faith. Quite a number of prayers spring from my own temperament and needs, particularly Numbers 23, 49, 52, 53. Number 66 was prayed on the day of my consecration, St John the Baptist's Day, 1963.

A wise spiritual writer has said: 'Tell me how a man prays and I can tell you what kind of man he is.' To make personal prayers available for others to read (and perhaps pray) is to expose one's inner self. There is a risk in doing so, but there may also be growth in self-knowledge and truth. That is the human side only; there may be a divine side as well, as expressed in the Collect for Purity in the Communion service. And it is possible that others may be helped, as two friends help one another when they speak heart to heart. That is my hope in sharing these prayers with a wider circle.

Open my eyes, O Lord,
that I may see the chariots of fire,
the crowd of watching angels and saints,
the four living creatures of creation,
the hosts of the redeemed,
from every nation and every generation,
and thyself, standing in the place of power,
directing thy Kingdom
and strengthening every struggling follower.
So seeing thee,
may I be held quiet and unafraid,
ready and daring, to be and do and bear
all that thy loving wisdom allows or wills,
O beloved Author and Finisher of my faith.

O God, I see signs of thy presence
    in every activity of men,
        expressions of beauty
    in the arts of men,
        principles of truth
    in the sciences of men,
        marks of nobility
    in ordinary lives.

O God, I see signs of thy presence
    in every place,
    in every bush,
    in every creature.

Thou art indeed
   the Fount of truth,
   the first Author of beauty,
   the Source of love,
   the Creator and Father of all,
     from all eternity
     to all eternity
ever the unchanging Self
   from whom our lesser selves derive
   in whom they find
     their Source and Goal.
Glory be to thee O God Eternal.

## REFLECTED GLORY                        3

Let me stand in thy presence, O God,
with the angels, and gaze
on the wonder of thy being
and the allness of thy love,
so that when I return
to the companionship of men,
there may be a recollection
of the real and the eternal
for me and for them.

## WALKING WITH GOD

Grant, O Lord,
that we may ever walk in thy presence,
with thy love in our hearts,
thy truth in our minds,
thy strength in our wills,
that when we finally stand before thee,
it may be with the assurance of thy welcome
and the joy of our homecoming.

## THE DIVINE WILL

O Lord my God,
thy will is holy, loving, and wise.
Let thy will be done in me,
for me, through me, in spite of me,
through him whose greatest joy
was to do thy will,
even Jesus Christ, my Lord.

## OUR BETHLEHEM

O God, we need a star
by which to set our journey through the world.
Help us to see in the baby born at Bethlehem
the eternal star which will lead us to the place
where truth and love and mercy meet.
So we may kneel with shepherds and kings
and find heart's joy and heart's peace
in Jesus Christ.

O Lord God,
I have learned more of truth from Jesus Christ
than from anyone else.
In the fallible records of his life, I have seen truth,
and in meditating upon them I have found
deeper and more personal truth.
In his movement within my being
I have experienced truth.
Thanks be to thee, O God, for Jesus Christ,
thy Word and thy Truth.


## THE MANY-SPLENDOURED GLORY 8

O Christ our God,
who art ever the same
yet revealest thyself anew to every seeker:
Thou art greater than our minds can grasp
or our words describe.
Knit us together in love and witness
that men may see thy many-splendoured glory
and may worship with us
the one Eternal God, blessed for evermore.

O Christ, my Lord,
set within my heart the law of self-giving love
which filled thy heart.
Let the love with which thou lovest me be in me
so that I may begin to love in thy way
in gratitude for thy love to me.


## BLESSINGS SHARED                                    10

O Lord Jesus Christ,
who hast commanded us to make known
the good news of thy love to all nations:
Help us so to experience
thy forgiveness, grace, and peace
that we may want all other people
to share those blessings
and to come into the family of thy Father,
to whom be all gratitude, love, and praise
for ever and ever.


## THE CROSS WITHIN MY HEART                           11

Grant, O Lord,
that I may know thy cross,
not only as standing on Golgotha,
but as planted within my heart,
whereby I know thee as the Son of God
who loved me and gave thyself for me,
that forgiven much and loving much,
I may ever abide in thy love.

## LOOKING AT THE PAST                                    12

Grant me, O Lord,
thy forgiveness and thy grace
that I may look back on the past
with a heart at peace and give thee
the thanks of a forgiven sinner,
redeemed through thy Son,
Jesus Christ, my Saviour.


## REMEMBERING THE PAST                                   13

O God,
who hast so faithfully cared for me in the past,
and so often seen me through to safety:
Grant me that in moments of depression,
desolation, failure, and despair,
I may look back in gratitude,
and refreshed by the remembrance of past grace
turn again to the future in renewed trust
and unfailing hope,
resting upon Jesus Christ,
my beloved Saviour.


## MY LIFE                                                14

Make me a good gardener, O Lord.
In the garden of my life,
let me sow seeds of life.
Let my words be good and fruitful.
Let my ideas be sound and fertile.
Let my actions be bright with holiness and love.

As far as lies within my power,
let me sow seeds of thy Kingdom,
and do thou, O Lord of life and growth,
make them germinate and produce
the promised harvest, O Lord of the hundredfold.


STUDY                                                   15

Grant, O Lord, I pray thee,
that from my study of thy Word
and the thoughts of other men,
my mind may be enlightened,
my conscience made sensitive,
my imagination fired,
and my will fortified
to love and serve thee with my whole being,
through Jesus Christ, my Lord.


A ROOM OF MY OWN                                        16

Within my inmost being, O Lord,
there is a chamber, locked and barred,
where thou hast never entered,
for I have kept it my very own.
Yet thou dost stand knocking and waiting,
and I cannot deafen my ears to thy knock
nor banish the silence of thy waiting.
O Lord, in fear and trembling I open the door,
lest when thou hast seen within, thou wilt not stay.
O my Lord, wilt thou indeed keep thy promise
and sup with me?

Lord, my thoughts turn in upon myself.
Turn them upward to thee
and outward to thy other children,
that I may forget myself,
and lose all fear and anxiety,
all self-seeking and self-consciousness,
in worship of thee and in love of others.
O save me from myself
to worship and love in perfect freedom.


## WHEN I AM HURT 18

O Lord, my God,
grant that when I am hurt,
I may stand before thee for healing;
when self-willed, come to thee for self-noughting;
when worried, lay my burden at thy feet
and find serenity and love,
O my Lord.


## 'DEPART FROM ME'? 19

O Holy Lord,
in the holiness of thy presence
my sinful nature cries out 'Depart'.
Yet if thou take me at my word
I am indeed lost and forsaken.

Come then, O Lord of holiness, Heavenly Guest,
enter now and cleanse the house of my soul
and abide with me for ever.


## UNDER MY ROOF? 20

Lord, I am not worthy
that thou shouldest come under my roof,
yet I know that I cannot live without thee.
Lord, I am sinful;
without thee I cannot become holy.
Lord, I am unloving;
come to my heart and waken it to love.
Lord, my heart is so small;
enlarge it, throw it open,
that I may welcome thee and make room
for all who come looking for love.


## IN DESPAIR OF SELF 21

O Lord God, I see my fellow men;
I know that I have a duty towards them.
I recognize the law of justice
that would restrain my selfish instincts:
I will keep from hurt, hatred, exploitation.
But of myself, I cannot love them.
Only if thou give me love can I love.
In despair of myself,
O Trinity of love, I ask for love.

O Christ our Lord,
   who wast in all things
   tempted as we are
Yet more searchingly and subtly
   by the spirit of evil
Trying to deflect thee
   from the perfect will of the Father;
Make clear to us his evil intent
   and deliver us from his power;
That as he found nothing in thee
   so he may gain no foothold in us
   who invoke thy victory and thy grace
   to be our rescue and our strength
   until the final triumph
      O Christ our Lord.


## THE TIGHT-ROPE                              23

Thou knowest, O Lord,
how often I have to walk the tight-rope
between truth and good will,
between one principle and another,
between one view and another,
between one person and another.
Let me ever keep my eye on thy truth and will,
and so walk without stumbling.
When I slip, let the net of thy love
catch me, lest I fall to damnation.

## FRIENDS OF THOMAS

O Risen and Ascended Christ,
whom not having seen we love:
We would touch the nail-marks in thy hands
and the spear-thrust to thy heart,
not for proof but for love.
Grant us the blessing promised
to those who have not seen yet believe,
until that eternal morning
when we shall see thee face to face
in thy glory, our Lord and our God.


## COALS OF FIRE

O God, thou hast forgiven me much
and my heart warms with love.
Thou hast accepted me
who am altogether unacceptable.
When I could not come to thee,
thou didst come to me.
O ever-forgiving God,
my heart knows its certainty of forgiveness,
and the fire of love begins to burn.
I will heap on it coals of gratitude
for sin forgiven—much sin,
until it blazes with love—much love—
for thee, my God.

O merciful God, I have been forgiven much
and I would love thee much.
Let me day by day realize more clearly
the hell of sin from which thou hast rescued me
and the Kingdom of love into which
thou hast brought me,
even the Kingdom of thy beloved Son,
Jesus Christ my Lord and Saviour.


AT A TIME OF TROUBLE                              27

O God, my heart is sore troubled,
full of longings that can find no words.
Let thy Spirit intercede within me
and lift my eyes to thee in trust and hope,
that thy will may be done in this situation.
Use me if there is aught that I can do,
and if I am not usable,
break me and mould me again,
closer to thy will. For his sake.


THE SAME ANGEL                                   28

O angel of temptation
    who didst strengthen my Lord
    in the wilderness.
O angel of the agony
    who didst strengthen my Lord
    in the garden.

Strengthen me in the hour of my temptation
   and in the hour of my death.
For the sake of him
   who conquered both sin and death,
   even Jesus Christ my Lord.


## THE HEART OF A CHILD

Grant me, O God,
   the heart of a child,
pure and transparent as a spring;
   a simple heart,
which never harbours sorrows;
a heart glorious in self-giving,
   tender in compassion;
a heart faithful and generous,
which will never forget any good
or bear a grudge for any evil.

   Make me a heart gentle and humble,
   loving without asking any return,
   largehearted and undauntable,
which no ingratitude can sour
and no indifference can weary;
   a heart penetrated by the love of Jesus
   whose desire will only be
      satisfied in heaven.

Grant me, O Lord,
   the mind and heart
   of thy dear Son.

O most holy and most adorable Spirit,
make me hear your soft and loving voice.
I would be before you as a light feather,
so that your breath
may carry me where it will,
and I never oppose to it the least resistance,
O most holy and adorable Spirit.


## SOUL OF MY SOUL                                    31

O Holy Spirit, soul of my soul,
I worship thee.
Enlighten me, guide me,
strengthen me, comfort me,
tell me what I should do, give me your orders.
I submit myself to all that you desire of me,
and all that you allow to happen to me.
Make me only to know your will,
O Holy Spirit.

O Holy Spirit, love of the Father and the Son,
establish thyself at the centre of our hearts,
and always lift our thoughts, our affections,
our activities, our actions,
like brightly burning flames,
to the bosom of the Father,
so that our entire life may be
a gloria to the Father, Son, and Holy Spirit.

## DISTURBER OF OUR PEACE 33

O Holy Spirit,
who dost so deeply disturb our peace:
Continue, we pray thee,
thy probings and promptings,
and goad us until we go thy way,
to our own greater blessing and deeper peace,
in Jesus Christ our Lord.

O Spirit of God,
speak to my spirit in thoughts that pierce
to the very centre of my being,
cutting through all pretence,
evasion, and misunderstanding,
with the rapier of truth,
so that I may know,
without the need to reason or explain.
Strengthen me from such moments
to live in truth.


## FREEDOM OF THE SPIRIT                         35

O Holy Spirit, whose presence is liberty:
Grant me that freedom of the Spirit,
which will not fear to tread in unknown ways,
nor be held back
by fear of others or misgivings of ourselves.
Ever beckon us forward
to the place of thy will
which is also the place of thy power,
O ever-leading, ever-loving Lord.

Grant, O my God,
that I may keep myself
under your loving hands,
so that you may complete
the work begun in me,
and make me more holy, more humble,
more loving, more dependent on you,
and more serviceable to you,
through Jesus Christ, my Saviour.

## THE DIVINE TOUCH 37

O Lord, let me be content
that I have felt thy touch upon my spirit.
Let me not think that I can hold thee
within the limits of my mind
or express thee fully in my words.
Rather let my whole bearing witness
that thou has touched me.

## THE ANCHOR 38

O Shepherd of souls,
the longer I live the more clearly I see
how men come to grief
through wrong desires, mistaken values,
and foolish hopes.
Continue in me thy compassion,
that through my touch with men

they may see the values of thy Kingdom,
and find in thee the anchor of their hopes,
and so never be shaken by the waves,
O Lord of the storm.


## DELIVER US FROM EVIL                                    39

O Lord and Master, who dost know us
more truly than we know ourselves:
Let thy Holy Spirit search out our weaknesses,
our fears, the unsurrendered things
within our souls,
that we may be saved from denial,
offence, disloyalty, and betrayal,
and be of whole heart
in our commitment to thee.


## FONTAL BEING                                            40

Give me a candle of the Spirit, O God,
as I go down into the deep of my own being.
Show me the hidden things.
Take me down to the spring of my life,
and tell me my nature and name.
Give me freedom to grow
so that I may become the self,
the seed which thou didst plant at my making.
Out of the deep I cry unto thee, O Lord.

O Spirit of God
   who dost speak to spirits
   created in thine own likeness:
   Penetrate into the depths of our spirits,
   into the storehouse of memories
   remembered and forgotten,
   into the depths of being,
   the very springs of personality.
   And cleanse and forgive
   making us whole and holy
   that we may be thine
   and live in the new being
     of Christ our Lord.


INNER LIFE                                      42

O Lord God, I thank thee
for the growing knowledge of myself,
of the depths of personality
which affect my thinking, my feeling,
my behaviour, and my dreams.
There is so much more than I ever thought,
so much more to offer thee
for the cleansing and sanctifying of thy Spirit.
Heal my inner divisions
in the unity of thy will;
set my fears at rest in the assurance
of thy love and grace;
let no resentments destroy my inner peace,
no thoughts of self deflect me
from thy purpose for me.

Help me to grow towards the fullness
of life and love seen in thy blessed Son,
Jesus Christ my Lord.


## SLEEP                                                        43

O God
who hast given me such a wonderful nature,
that even when I sleep
my mind continues to think,
giving me understanding of myself
and clues how to live:
Help me to know my inner self and to trust it,
for it is there that thy Spirit works.
I praise thee, my God and Maker,
who dost give gifts to thy loved ones,
even while we sleep.


## DREAMS                                                       44

O God,
who through thy ordering of our inner nature
dost show us truths about ourselves as we sleep:
Help us to interpret these messages
from the depths of our being,
and to know and accept ourselves
as the starting-point for growth
towards the pattern of thy Son,
Jesus Christ our Lord.

O God,
help me to search out my heart and mind,
to find that which interests and thrills me most,
that to which I most joyfully respond
from within or from without.
And as I search,
grant that I may discover that I belong to thee
and begin to love thee with all my being,
O Lord my God.


IMAGES 46

O Christ, my Lord, again and again
I have said with Mary Magdalene,
'They have taken away my Lord
and I know not where they have laid him.'
I have been desolate and alone.
And thou hast found me again, and I know
that what has died is not thou, my Lord,
but only my idea of thee,
the image which I have made to preserve
what I have found, and to be my security.
I shall make another image, O Lord,
better than the last.
That too must go, and all successive images,
until I come to the blessed vision of thyself,
O Christ, my Lord.

O Lord, when I call others to pray,
teach me to pray,
lest when I have preached to others
I myself should be a man without prayer.
Strengthen me in a discipline of prayer.
Deepen my faith in prayer.
Enlarge my vision of thy Church
as a fellowship of prayer.
If it be for thy glory and my good,
let me see thee answering prayer.
And let my prayer be always in the Name
of Jesus, thy Son, my Lord.


RENEWAL                                                      48

O my God,
grant that I may so wait upon thee,
that when quick decision and action are needed
I may mount up with wings as an eagle;
and when under direction of thy will
and the needs of men
I have to keep going under pressure,
I may run and not be weary;
and in times of routine and humble duty
I may walk and not faint.
For all my fresh springs are in thee,
O God of my strength.

## INNER PEACE

Dear Lord, quieten my spirit
and fix my thoughts on thy will,
that I may see what thou wouldest have done,
and contemplate its doing
without self-consciousness,
without inner excitement,
without haste and without delay,
without fear of other people's judgements
or anxiety about success,
knowing only that it is thy will
and must therefore be done quietly,
faithfully, and lovingly,
for in thy will alone is our peace.


## READY FOR BURNING

O Holy Spirit, help me to submit to thy fire,
that all that is not holy may be burnt,
and all that is not eternal may be destroyed.
Help me to hold myself in the fire
until all that is foreign is consumed,
and I burn with the bright, painless flame
of thy presence.


## THE HIDDEN CHRIST

O Eternal Lord Christ, we praise thee
that since the beginning of the universe
thou didst work unrecognized
as the wisdom and light of men.

We praise thee that thy Name
became known in a human life,
in the humility of Bethlehem,
the love of Calvary,
and the glory of resurrection.
Help us to see thee working
in everything that is true, holy, and loving,
and grant that we may delight
to work humbly and unrecognized,
desiring only that thy loving purpose
shall go forward, until all come
to see thee as the hidden heart of all things.


EVER PRESENT                                    52

O Lord my God,
there are times when my heart is cold
and I cannot feel thee near,
days when all that keeps me going
is a sense of duty.
Keep me steady and faithful at these times
and remind me of thy presence in the past,
until suddenly
thou dost make thyself known to me again,
and I know how the grass feels
when the dew falls,
and the bird at the day's first ray of light.
Then I realize that I have walked by faith,
safely, because thou hast been with me
all the time.

O my Lord, when moods
of depression, anxiety, or resentment
take possession of me,
let me ask, 'Why art thou so heavy, O my soul,
and why art thou so disquieted within me?'
And let the answer show me
the cause of my mood and dispel it,
so that I forget my hurts and want only thee.


BURN! BURN! BURN!                          54

O God, who art a consuming fire
of holiness and love:
Burn me until all evil is consumed,
all selfishness, all impurity, all unlove,
that I may worship in thy presence
and at last be granted
the blessing of the pure in heart
to see thee in thy holiness,
through Jesus Christ my Lord.


THE FIRES OF LUST                          55

O God, who in holiness and love
dost look down upon the sins
and perversions of men:
Grant that thy Church may proclaim
the gospel of thy forgiveness and grace,
to all in the power of lust
and to all who exploit the weakness of others.

Give us love, courage, and wisdom
in our efforts to help them,
and burn up in us all impurity.
We ask this for the holiness and love
of Jesus Christ, our blessed Lord.


## SAINTLINESS 56

O Lord, who in every age dost reveal thyself
to the childlike and lowly of heart,
and from every race dost write names
in thy book of life:
Give us the simplicity and faith of thy saints,
that loving thee above all things,
we may be what thou wouldest have us be
and do what thou wouldest have us do.
So may we be numbered with thy saints
and enter with them into eternal joy and glory,
through Jesus Christ our Lord.


## NOT FOR MY SUCCESS 57

O Lord God,
I see that all thou doest for me
is for my own good,
my own cleansing and strengthening,
and not for my success
nor even for the good I can do to others.
Thy hands are constantly fashioning me.
Help me to keep myself under thy hands
that one day I may be an instrument
for thy use.

## MY CHIEFEST GOOD

O my God, thou art my chiefest good,
the greatest blessing in my life.
With thee so close I have no fear.
Even my body feels safe,
undismayed at the thought of death.
For thou wilt show me the way of life,
and give me the full joy of thy presence.
To have thee close is the foretaste of heaven,
O God, my God.

## GOD IN CREATION

Lead us, O God,
from the sight of the lovely things of the world
to the thought of thee their Creator;
and grant that delighting
in the beautiful things of thy creation
we may delight in thee,
the first author of beauty
and the Sovereign Lord of all thy works,
blessed for evermore.

## FAITH IN GOD'S WORKING

O God, who hast created the universe
and art ever at work in it
to restore the harmony
broken by the self-will of men:
Give us quiet, confident, joyful faith in thee,
that our eyes may ever look in expectation

to thy love and power,
rather than to the power of evil
or to the weakness of men.
Help us to stand firm in the assurance
that thou art at work in all that happens,
in the foolishness and rebellion of men
as well as in their efforts for goodness,
turning all to thy loving purpose.
Fill us with joy and hope in believing,
through him who was victorious
over sin, enmity, defeat, and death,
even Jesus Christ, our beloved Lord.


ORIGINAL GOODNESS                          61

O God, I praise thee
for the goodness and love in ordinary people.
There is much weakness and much sin,
and often downright evil,
but also much
love, courage, and cheerfulness.
O Lord most holy,
people are not far from thy Kingdom.
Draw them in, O Christ,
by thine own goodness and love.

O Lord God, we thank thee
that thy Spirit is ever urging the spirits of men
to higher achievements of wisdom, skill,
love, and goodness.
We praise thee for the developing universe,
by obeying whose laws
men can circle the earth and reach the stars.
Grant thy wisdom and protection
to those who would go still further,
and help them to know
that they can never overtake thee
nor pass out of thy care,
through thy perfect Son,
Jesus Christ, our Lord.


GUILELESS                                                 63

O God,
    for the sake of Nathaniel,
        grant me a childlike spirit
        free from guile and self-seeking;
    that my eyes may be open to see
        the ladder between heaven and earth
            even Jesus Christ my Lord.

Grant, O Lord, that thy Spirit
may permeate every sphere of thought and action.
Let those who believe in thee
take with them into their daily work
the values of thy Kingdom,
the insights of the gospel
and the love of their fellow men.
Hasten the time
when justice and brotherhood shall be established,
and when all men shall be brought
into the unity of thy Son,
our Saviour Jesus Christ.


MUSTARD SEED 65

O Lord
    let the seed of thy Kingdom
    be in me
    and let it grow
until it becomes a tree
    of refreshment and love
under which men may shelter.

O Lord God,
keep me humble, make me holy,
fill me with faith and love,
grant me wisdom to know thy will
and grace to carry it out to thy glory,
through Jesus Christ my Lord.


INTERCESSION                                            67

Lord, let me be a mirror
made clean and bright by thy forgiveness,
held up to thy glory,
that I may reflect thy life and love
to those for whom I pray.


BEFORE PRAYER                                           68

O Holy Spirit,
be with us in this time of prayer,
and grant us living touch with thee.
Give us the insights of thy Kingdom,
the vision of thy purpose,
the guidance of thy wisdom,
and grace to be fellow-workers with thee
in the doing of thy just and loving will,
through Jesus Christ our Lord.

O God, I thank thee for life and being,
and for all the blessings of the past day;
for the love that I have received and given,
for all the kindnesses received from others,
and for thy grace going before me
and following after me.
Above all I thank thee
for him through whom I know of thy love
and receive thy grace,
even Jesus Christ, my Lord and Saviour.


AT THE PULPIT STEPS                            70

O Lord, I feel no confidence
in what I have prepared.
I have no confidence in myself
and no warm sense of thy presence with me.
I go in bare faith and cold will,
because you push me.


AFTER PREACHING                                71

Follow after me, O Lord,
and blot from the memories of those who heard,
all that was not of thy will,
all that was mistaken,
self-willed, or self-regarding.
Fertilize any seed of thy Word,
that it may bear some fruit
in them and in me.

Be pleased, O Lord, to remember
my friends, all that have prayed for me,
and all that have done me good.
Do thou good to them,
and return their kindness
double into their bosom,
rewarding them with blessings,
sanctifying them with grace,
and bringing them at last to thy glory.


STILL IN THY HAND 73

O God, Creator and Father of all:
We know that those whom we love
and who have died are still in thy hand
in the world of spirit.
Grant them, O Lord, courage and grace
that they may grow into that likeness
which is thy will for them.
And when we die, grant that our loved ones
may be there to welcome us
to that spiritual country
which is our true home,
through Jesus Christ our Lord.

O Lord God, thou knowest
how much the souls of the departed
need thy cleansing and forgiveness,
before they feel at home in thy presence.
Grant that in the clearer light of Paradise
they may see their need and accept the grace
thou hast been offering them
since the moment of their creation.
So, most gracious God,
thou wilt be their Redeemer
as well as their Creator,
and all through Jesus Christ, our Lord.

## A GLORIOUS BODY 75

O God, who hast shown us
by the resurrection of Jesus Christ
that the whole of man's life
shall be redeemed and transformed:
We thank thee that in him
our bodies shall be transformed and glorified
as his glorious body.
Grant us so to discipline and use them now
that they may more perfectly become
the instrument of our spirit,
prepared for eternal life.
Through him, who died and was buried
and now lives and reigns with thee in glory,
ever our Saviour Jesus Christ.

O God, rouse thy Church, lest we sleep and miss men's
   need of thee and thy yearning love for men.
O God, cleanse thy Church and forgive our lack of zeal
   for thy Kingdom.
O God, set thy Church ablaze with the fire of thy
   Spirit, that we may spend and be spent for thy gospel,
   thy will, and thy glory,
       through all our days.


FOR UNITY                                              77

O Lord Jesus Christ,
thy body was broken on the cross
by the sin of the world.
Thy body is broken now
by the sins of the Church.
Forgive the world the sins it knew not,
and make the Church know the sin
it is doing to thee.
Bring us all to penitence and unity in thee,
for the world's sake.

O Christ our Lord, we are one in thee.
We have all been saved by thee.
In Baptism we have all been admitted
into thy new creation.
In Communion we are all fed by thee.
Yet, O Christ, we are divided.
Draw us closer to thee,
so that we come closer to one another.
Make us one according to thy will
and in the way that thou thyself shalt choose.


FOR THE FULLNESS OF THE CHURCH        79

O thou who didst create light pure and clear,
yet refracted into the colours of the rainbow:
Grant that we, who see thee
each from our own vision,
may in sharing our experience with one another
see thee more nearly as thou art
in all thy truth and beauty.
Let each Church bring its heritage
of truth and worship
that the full inheritance may be revealed
and made available for all who call thee Father,
through him in whom thy fullness dwells,
even thy Eternal Son, Jesus Christ our Lord.

Lord of the Church,
it is only with thy authority
that men dare proclaim thy gospel
and be ministers of thy sacraments,
bringing to thy people
the cleansing, life-giving water of Baptism
and the bread and wine
of the soul's health and joy.
Save us from arrogating to ourselves
the rights of thy love;
help us to be humble instruments of thy grace.
For thou art the great High Priest,
the Shepherd of souls,
and the Saviour of all,
and to thee be the glory for ever and ever.


AN UNDERSTANDING HEART 81

Grant me, O Lord, an understanding heart,
that I may see into the hearts of thy people,
and know their strengths and weaknesses,
their hopes and despairs,
their efforts and failures,
their need of love and their need to love.
Through my touch with them
grant comfort and hope, and the assurance
that new life begins at any age and on any day,
redeeming the past, sanctifying the present,
brightening the future with thy unfailing love,
brought to me in Jesus Christ,
thy Son, my Lord.

## A SUFFICIENT PRAYER 82

Lord, he whom thou lovest is sick.
Do for him according to his need, dear Lord.


## A TRUSTING PRAYER 83

O God, the Creator and Father of all,
we praise thee that thy will
is life, health, and strength.
Help all who are ill or in pain
to place themselves in thy hands in loving trust,
so that thy healing life may
make them well and strong,
able and ready to do thy holy will,
through him who has made known to us
both thy love and thy will,
even Jesus Christ our Lord.


## FOR THE SICK IN MIND 84

O Holy Spirit who dost delve into all things,
even the deep things of God
and the deep things of man,
we pray thee to penetrate the springs of personality
of all who are sick in mind,
to bring them cleansing, healing, and unity.
Sanctify all memory, dispel all fear,
bring them to love thee
with all their mind and will,
that they may be made whole
and glorify thee for ever.

We ask this in the Name of him
who cast out devils and healed men's minds,
even Jesus Christ our Lord.

## FOR THE HALLOWING OF SUFFERING 85

O Lord we pray thee for all weighed down
with the mystery of suffering.
Reveal thyself to them as the God of love
who thyself dost bear all our sufferings.
Grant that they may know
that suffering borne in fellowship with thee
is not waste or frustration,
but can be turned to goodness and blessing
greater than if they had never suffered,
through him who on the cross suffered
rejection and hatred, loneliness and despair,
agonizing pain and physical death,
and rose victorious from the dead,
conquering and to conquer,
even Jesus Christ, our Lord.

O Almighty and Everlasting God,
we praise thee for teaching us
through the cross and resurrection of thy Son
that suffering can be a creative force.
Grant, we pray thee,
that as his humiliation won glory and life,
so our sufferings and endurance
may bring his presence and his power
into a needy world,
through the same Jesus Christ our Lord.


'INCURABLES'                                                87

O Heavenly Father,
we pray thee for those suffering
from diseases at present incurable.
Give them the victory of trust and hope,
that they may never lose their faith
in thy loving purpose.
Grant thy wisdom to all who are working
to discover the secrets of disease,
and the faith that through thee
all things are possible.
We ask this in the Name of him
who went about doing good
and healing all kinds of disease,
even thy Son Jesus Christ our Lord.

Hasten the time, O Lord,
when no man shall live in contentment
while he knows that others have need.
Inspire in us and in people of all nations
the desire for social justice,
that the hungry may be fed,
the homeless welcomed, the sick healed,
and a just order established in the world,
according to thy gracious will
made known in Jesus Christ, our Lord.


A GREAT HAPPENING                                              89

O God, we thank thee
that the nations are learning
the compassion of our Lord, Jesus Christ.
Grant that our nation
may give generously for the relief of the homeless
and that our people may welcome the refugee.
Help us in our plenty
to remember the needs of others
and never to grudge the cost of helping them;
for his sake who did not grudge the cross,
but gave himself for all,
even Jesus Christ, our Lord.

O merciful and loving Father of all,
look down, we pray thee,
on the hungry millions in the world to-day
who are at the mercy of disease.
Grant that we who live
so comfortably and gently
may have true sympathy with them
and do all in our power to help them
to that abundant life which is thy will;
through Jesus Christ our Lord.

O God, I pray
   for bread for the hungry
   homes for the homeless
   peace for the fearful
   healing for the sick
   love for the hard of heart
   life for the departed
     and Christ for all.

Pour thy blessing, O God, we pray thee,
upon Elizabeth our Queen,
that she may fulfil her calling
as a Christian ruler.
Support her in the ceaseless round of duty,
inspire her in the service of many peoples,
give her wise and selfless ministers,
bless her in home and family,
and grant that through her
the Commonwealth may be knit together
in one great brotherhood,
a strength and joy to all its members
and an instrument of thy wise and loving will,
through Jesus Christ our Lord.


## ATOMIC ENERGY                                    93

O God of all wisdom and power,
who art ever revealing thyself
to those who seek for thee:
Grant that as men discover
the secrets of thy universe,
they may use them according to thy will,
not for destruction and war,
but for the welfare of all thy people.
We ask this in the Name of Jesus Christ our Lord.

Grant us, O Lord,
to see our aborigine and coloured countrymen
as equally with us the children of thy love
for whom also Christ died,
and to welcome them into our national life,
receiving from them gifts we may have lost.
Free us from racial pride and colour prejudice,
indifference and desire for apartness,
and include us in the new humanity
of thy beloved son Jesus Christ,
Universal Brother to us all.


## IMMIGRANTS                                95

O God, our Creator and Redeemer,
who didst send thy Son
to gather all men into thy love:
Grant that thy Church may be truly his Body,
and by its ministry
to those who come to live in our land
may show forth his love
and forward his purpose,
through the same Jesus Christ our Lord.

O God, I thank thee
for all the creatures thou hast made,
so perfect in their kind —
great animals like the elephant and the rhinoceros,
humorous animals like the camel and the monkey,
friendly ones like the dog and the cat,
working ones like the horse and the ox,
timid ones like the squirrel and the rabbit,
majestic ones like the lion and the tiger,
for birds with their songs.
O Lord give us such love for thy creation,
that love may cast out fear,
and all thy creatures see in man
their priest and friend,
through Jesus Christ our Lord.

O God, whose will it is
that men should rest from their labours
and find refreshment of body, mind, and spirit:
We thank thee for our yearly holidays
and for our weekly day of rest.
Bless all those now on holiday,
help them to enjoy more fully
the beauty of countryside and sea
and the message of historic places.

Give them happy fellowship
and wholesome jollity,
and grant that they may not forget thee,
the Creator of the natural world
and the Father of all that live,
ever working thy purposes of love,
through Jesus Christ, thy Son, our Lord.


FOR THE WORLD'S SAKE                           98

O Lord Christ, for the world's sake
    Thou didst stand against the world;
Grant that I too
    may stand for the world
    against the world,
And love the world
    with something of thy great love.

O God, who by the leading of a star
didst draw men of old
to the stable at Bethlehem:
Mercifully grant that by the operation
of the same Holy Spirit
men may find in their own religions
some clue which shall lead them
to see in Christ the goal of their hopes
and to worship him
as Saviour and Lord of all.


## THANKSGIVING FOR THE BUDDHA                    100

O God, who art the Creator of all worlds
and the Lord of all ages,
I praise thee for the Buddha
who taught men that desire, greed, and attachment
were the causes of men's misery.
I thank thee for his teaching
of the noble eightfold path
which men should tread
and for his compassion for all that has life.
Grant that those who follow him as teacher
may find his wisdom confirmed
in thy Word Jesus Christ, through whom
they may receive forgiveness and saving grace,
strength to live the good life
and finally by thy mercy
the enjoyment of eternal life in thy heaven,
through the same Jesus Christ our Lord.

O God, I pray thee for my fellow men
   who believe the world of nature
     to be indwelt by spirits,
   who see in the life of the spring
     and the tree
     and the fertility of the soil
   the action of spiritual beings.

Grant that they may come to know thee
   as the Spirit of holiness and love,
and be delivered from all fear
   to worship thee
with the love and reverence of sons,
   through Jesus Christ our Lord.


FOR HINDUS                                          102

O God, I thank thee
that thou hast revealed to our Hindu brethren
that their spirits are akin to thy divine Spirit.
Lead them and us, we pray thee,
from the unreal to the real,
from darkness to light,
and from death to immortality,
through thy incarnate Son,
Jesus Christ our Lord.

O Lord Jesus Christ, Eternal God,
    who didst send forth thy apostles
        in the threefold Name
    to preach the gospel to every creature:
We pray thee for Muslims in every land.
We thank thee for their faithfulness
    to the divine unity and majesty,
and we pray that by the wisdom of thy Spirit,
they may be brought to know
    the eternal relationship of love
        within the Godhead,
and see in thee the full and perfect Word of God,
    who livest and reignest
    in the unity of the Godhead,
    blessed for evermore.


## FOR COMMUNISTS                                104

O Christ, who in thyself are both the gospel
    and the Kingdom,
show us how to preach good news
    to those who fight for the kingdom of this world.
Help us to proclaim thy love for them
and call them in to work for the new heaven and earth
    which comes down from heaven,
so that both they and we may rejoice in thy Kingdom
    of righteousness, peace, and joy, which has no end,
        and worship the God who never fails,
even our Creator and Saviour, blessed for evermore.

O eternal Word,
   who from the beginning hast revealed
   glimpses of truth and righteousness
   through prophets of many faiths:
We praise thee
   that all that is of value
     is found fulfilled and perfected in thee,
   and all that is mistaken
   finds its correction
     in thee.
Do thou draw all seekers of truth and righteousness
   to thyself,
and vouchsafe to them the unsearchable riches
   that we have found in thee, dear Lord.


PERSONAL ENCOUNTER                      106

O Spirit of God, guide me
as I seek to discover thy working
with men of other faiths.
Give me the strength of truth,
the gentleness and strength of love,
the clear eye of judgement, and the courage of faith.
Above all, grant me a deeper understanding
of him who is the Truth,
a greater commitment to him who is the Lord,
a deeper gratitude to him
who is the Saviour of all,
even Jesus Christ thy Eternal Word,
through whom thou art drawing all men
to thyself, that they may be saved for ever,

and worship thee the only God
blessed for evermore.


## THE SPIRIT OF ENCOUNTER

O Eternal Lord God,
Creator and Saviour of all,
I pray thee to guide me with thy Spirit
as I meet men of other faiths.
Grant me friendliness to gain their confidence,
eagerness to listen, and wisdom to understand.
Help me to speak
without self-consciousness or self-assertion
of my faith and what thou hast done for me.
Guard me against all compromise with truth,
give me the penetrating insight of thy Word,
quick to discern the inmost thoughts of the heart.
Let me not presume to defend thee
who didst put thyself at the mercy of men
at Bethlehem and Calvary.
Invest me with thine own love for all I meet,
give me a word to forward thy purpose for each.
And ever purify my faith and worship,
that I may become more wholly thine,
through Jesus Christ, my Lord and Saviour,
the Lord and Saviour of all.

O Christ, my Way
   to the God of all salvation,
Men of other faiths
   believe they have their own salvation faith.
Be with them, dear Lord,
   to encourage them on their way
   to their own Jerusalem
so that we all find ourselves
   with the spirits of just men made perfect
   with the saints of every age and faith
in the presence of the Eternal God
   the God of many names
Creator, Lover, Saviour of us all.

# Prayed in Jerusalem

## HOLY PEOPLE

O Eternal Lord God, Source of all truth, Lover of all
men, we thank thee for the experience of living in this
city. Grant that we may be
    humble, grateful people,
    worshipping people,
    holy people,
Help us to be peace-loving people
    who know the things that belong to peace,
    who pray and work for peace,
    who try to understand the experiences, the hurts, the
    hopes of people from whom we differ.
Let this city be a centre of unity for the Churches.
Let it be a place of friendship and understanding for
    men of different faiths.
Let it be truly the City of Peace, a joy of the whole earth
    and a place of blessing to all nations.
For the sake of him who wept in love over this city and
    died in love outside its walls,
The Everliving One, ever present with thee to heal and
    bless, Jesus Christ our blessed Lord.

O Christ our Lord, thou didst weep over this city,
   because the people in it did not know the things that
   make for peace.
Grant to us who live in it today to know these things—
   truth, justice, and love—to hold them in mind and
   heart, and to work for them in word and deed, so that
   we may be sons of peace and brothers of thine, O
   Prince of Peace, Christ our Lord.


BETHLEHEM                                        111

O God, in thine infinite mercy look on the travail of the
   human race—fear, hatred, war, hunger, homelessness,
   grief, and anxiety.

Thou art among them, O Lord, as thou wast in the
   homeless babe in this place of the manger.

Move the hearts of nations and governments to use thy
   gifts of wealth and skill to build the Kingdom of thy
   love, where all shall live free from fear and free from
   want, free from hatred, cruelty, and sin, free to look
   into the faces of our fellow men with welcome and love.

O Father, we are all brothers and sisters of the babe born
   in this place—wise men, simple shepherds, the tired
   and the old, the young and the strong, the sad and the
   lonely, the hungry and the homeless, the living and the
   dead, men of every race and religion.

May all come to gaze with us at the humble, defenceless
   love of the perennial Bethlehem, the recurrent spring-
   time of the human spirit which renews our faith, our

hope, our love, our life, in the knowledge of thy
eternal goodness, O Lord our God.


THE HOLY LAND                                           112

O Lord our God, we would hold close to thee this land
    with its problems, tensions, hatreds, and griefs.

We lift hearts and minds to thee in faith that when we
    pray with loving persistence thou wilt work with
    unfailing love, and things will change in the direction
    of thy will.

Increase our faith, our hope, our love, so that we may
    be channels of healing, reconciliation, and blessing,

for the sake of him who was incarnate in this land and
    gave his life in this city, and who is omnipresent with
    thee in love, power, and glory,
        even Jesus Christ the Saviour of all.


AT THE FEET WASHING                                     113

Lord,
    I keep on thinking
    how I may wash
    the feet of others,
    not seeing thee
    kneeling before me
        waiting
    to wash my feet.

# SHARING HIS LIFE

## Personal Devotions for Holy Communion

At first sight these devotions may seem to be a para-phrased summary of the Prayer Book Service, which can only be used as a substitute for the set prayers said by priest or people. They are not meant to be this, but can be used in two ways.

First of all, in preparation before the service, either at home or in church. Few people would be able to use the whole of this devotional material at one time, but many might be helped by studying and praying two or three of the prayers beforehand, to register the devotional content, and use it in a flash of remembrance when these items occur in the course of the service.

Secondly, these devotions might be used as a parallel and accompanying exercise of worship. The eyes can take in very quickly the devotional thought suggested, and the mind and heart can infuse it into the familiar words. In this way, attention need not be distracted from the service, but can become more clearly concentrated.

There are natural pauses in the service, for example while the altar book is being moved or the offertory presented. In particular there is the long silence while the congregation is receiving Communion. Many people are at a loss to know how to employ this time. Instead of forming a long queue before Communion, or vaguely turning over the pages of the prayer book after Communion, there is suggested a plan of detailed and loving intercession, which could be creative and redemptive in the life of the one who prays and in the lives of those for whom he prays.

The Acts of Preparation and Thanksgiving are not long in words, but they are expandable in meditation and devotion. Unhurried approach in preparation and an unhurrying lingering in thanksgiving could make more real this sacrament of our Lord's presence and the sharing of his life.

# Prayers in Preparation

In remembrance of thee, dear Lord          114
    The humble birth at Bethlehem
    the quiet years at Nazareth
    the ministry in Galilee and Jerusalem:
        In remembrance of thee.

    Thy readiness to face death
    thine unfailing love
    thy forgiveness:
        In remembrance of thee

    The rejection by thy people
    thy body nailed to the cross
    the spiritual loneliness:
        In remembrance of thee

    The finishing of thy task
    thy commendation to the Father
    the rending of body and spirit:
        In remembrance of thee

    The triumph over evil
    the acceptance of death
    the glory of resurrection:
        In remembrance of thee

    Thy return to the Father
    thy reign in heaven
    thine unceasing intercession:
        In remembrance of thee

The realization of the Spirit
his sevenfold gift
his harvest within:
    In remembrance of thee, dear Lord.


O my Lord and God                           115
   the journey is too great for me
   unless
      thou feed me with bread from heaven
        and wine of life
   unless
      thou share with me thine own life
        victorious over sin,
        hatred, pain, and death.
Let thy blood
   flow through my veins
   thy strength
   be my strength
   thy love
   be my love
   And the father's will
   be my will as well as thine
Let me be one with thee
   in heart, mind, and will.
      O Lord, my God.

O Creator God                                116
   I come to thee for life
     Have mercy upon me.

O Redeemer God
   I come to thee for forgiveness
     Have mercy upon me.

O Indwelling God
   I come to thee for grace
     Have mercy upon me.

O Triune God
   I come in worship and love
     Have mercy upon me.

                                         117

O Christ my Lord, I thank thee that in the hour of
danger thou didst think of me and all thy followers
down the ages

   and in this sacrament, didst leave us a remembrance
   of thy love, a sharing of thy life, and part in thy
   sacrifice of loving obedience to thy Father and our
   Father.

I come, O Lord, in loving remembrance and in grateful
participation, in company with all who love thee in
every place and in every generation.

   O Eternal Saviour, O Source of life.

## AT THE COLLECT FOR PURITY

There is not a thought in my mind,
not a word on my lips,
not a secret deed of kindness or of shame
which thou dost not know, O Lord my God.
Let me stand in thy presence and be cleansed,
sanctified, and vitalized by thy Holy Spirit,
through Jesus Christ, my Master and Lord.


## AT THE READING OF THE LAW

Sweeter than honey, more precious than gold
are thy commands, O holy and righteous God—
a light to my feet, wisdom to my mind,
incentive to my will, joy to my heart.
Grant that I may put thee first,
before all other people however dear,
above all other things however precious.
Then I shall love all else rightly and fully.
O my God, I have no good beyond thee.


## AT THE COLLECT

O God, I pray this ancient prayer
with him who first prayed it,
with thy people who pray it year by year,
and with all brethren who pray it to-day.
Amen.
Let it be so!
Amen.

Let this letter be addressed to me,
O Lord Christ,
from those who were near thee in time and space.
Let me come nearer to thee through their words.
And be to me what thou wast to them.

Christ Jesus,
my faith reaches back for authentic touch
with thy visit to mankind.
I would touch thy hands, look into thy face,
hear thy voice, discover thy meaning.
I have not seen, O my Lord and my God,
but I believe.
Bless me with thy living touch to-day.

Let me recite, O God,
the great things thou hast done:
in creation, in the coming of Jesus,
in his life and death of love,
in his resurrection of power,
in his ascension of glory;
in the indwelling of thy Spirit,
in the existence of thy Church,
in the continuance of revelation,
in forgiveness, in Baptism,
in the fellowship of believers

across all barriers of time and space,
of life and death, of earth and heaven;
in the promise of eternal life.
Let me never weary in telling of
thy wondrous works,
O God of eternity and love.


## AT THE COLLECTION 124

O Lord, thy Church must be maintained
to carry on the serving, saving work
of thy dear Son.
Thy ministers must be maintained.
Thy children in many lands and in many needs
must be helped.
Accept this gift of my money,
with my deepening gratitude and growing love,
as a pledge that I will work with thee
for thy will and thy Kingdom,
in obedience to Jesus Christ my Lord.


## AT THE OFFERTORY 125

O Creator God, we offer thee this bread and this wine,
    symbols of thy creative power in nature.
O Creator God, we offer thee this bread and this wine,
    tokens of the labours of men.
We offer them to thee in gratitude, and in faith that
    thou wilt give them back to us, enriched to nourish
    and refresh our spirits.
We bless thee for the universe, the order of nature,
    our dependence on our fellow men for physical food,

and our dependence on thee for spiritual life.

Bless the Lord, O my soul, and all that is within me, bless his holy Name.

## AT THE PRAYER FOR THE CHURCH 126

O God, I thank thee for the Church of thy dear Son, without which I would not know of thy love.

Without which I would not be caught up in worship.

Without which I would be lonely and afraid.

Without which I would not know of forgiveness and grace.

Without which I would not be constantly reminded that I am thy child, called to live the Christ-life.

I pray for the Church, that it may be one according to thy will;
that it may be holy in all its members and in all its branches;
that it may be catholic—for all men and in all truth;
that it may be apostolic in faith and in outgoing love.

O God, make the Church truly the Body of thy Son, a community of love and service, a pioneer of salvation.

Lord, I have sinned
  against thee
  against others
  against myself

Lord, I have sinned
  against the law
  against thy light
  against thy love

Lord, I have sinned
  in thought
  in word
  in deed
  in omission

Lord, I have fallen short
  of thy will for me
  of thy glory for me

And again and again
  seventy times seven
Thou dost say
  my sins are forgiven me
    O gracious, loving Lord.

The veil of the Temple is torn from top to bottom,
The way is open to thy presence.

I follow thy Son, the High Priest of all mankind, into
the Holy of Holies.

I kneel with angels and archangels
with saints and martyrs
and the forgiven of all generations,
with the whole Church

And hear their Holy, Holy, Holy,
And cry Amen! Amen!


## AT THE PRAYER OF HUMBLE ACCESS 129

I am not worthy
to kneel in the outermost rank
O Holy Lord.

Yet I have been brought here
by thy Son,
my Lord.

Abba, Father,
I have come home
with him.

Let him live in me
and I in him
O merciful Lord.

I remember
 the night when he was betrayed
 the night before he accepted death
 the night when his hour was come
 as loving and defenceless as the night of his birth.

How he washed their feet
 and gave the new command
 and broke bread. . .
 and blessed wine. . .

And gave them and us
 a sacrament of his continuing presence
 a sharing of his own life
 I remember, I remember.


AT THE GIVING OF THE PEACE                    131

O Christ, who didst often bless thy disciples
with the greeting *'Shalom'*,
wishing them peace of heart,
well-being and blessing:
We thank thee for this prayer and gift,
and we pass it on to our fellow disciples
in word and touch, not only in liturgy
but in every activity of our common life,
 O Lord of Peace,
 O Giver of Grace,
 O Blessing from the Eternal Father,
 God of us all.

Lord, as I kneel at thy table
  with my fellow men
  Let me be brother
  to them all.

Lord, let thy life within me
  keep me grateful
          loving
          humble
          holy
  today, tomorrow, and always

Bread of heaven—
  strength, courage, love
  sufficient for every need

Wine of heaven—
  cleansing, refreshing, gladdening,
  the cup of blessing

My Lord and my Life
  I can never thank thee enough
  never love thee enough.


AT THE SILENCE                    133

O Lord, I remember
  all my loved ones
  living and departed . . . . . . . . . . . . . . . . . . . . . . . . . . . . .

O Lord, I remember
  all in need of thy love . . . . . . . . . . . . . . . . . . . . . . . . . .

O Lord, I remember
  all my brethren in thy Church . . . . . . . . . . . . . . . . . .

Lord, I bring before thee
  every duty . . . . . . . . . . . . . . . . . . . . . . . . . . . . . . . . . . .
  every problem . . . . . . . . . . . . . . . . . . . . . . . . . . . . . . . .
  every opportunity . . . . . . . . . . . . . . . . . . . . . . . . . . . .

Lord, I ask thy grace
  for my home . . . . . . . . . . . . . . . . . . . . . . . . . . . . . . . . . .
  for my work . . . . . . . . . . . . . . . . . . . . . . . . . . . . . . . . . .
  for every relationship . . . . . . . . . . . . . . . . . . . . . . . . . .

Remake me
  in thy likeness
    O Christ my Lord.


## AT THE LORD'S PRAYER                                     134

With thy perfect Son
  we come to thee
  and say '*Abba*, Father!'

With all thy children
  we come
  and say, 'Our Father'.

We want thy Kingdom
  thy will
  thy glory.

Strengthen and feed us,
  *Abba*, Father. Father, dear Father.

Lord God,
   in return for thy great love
I would bring an offering,
But there is only one worthy offering
The perfect obedience of thy Son
   even unto death.

Lord God,
   I remember that offering,
   I plead it before thee,

And though it be all-sufficient
   I add to it
   the offering of myself,
   body, mind, and spirit,
   mind, heart, and will,
   all that I have,
   all that I am,
   all that by thy grace I can become.

Accept, O Lord God,
   this unworthy sacrifice
   and cleanse
   and sanctify
      and use it
in the service of thy Kingdom
   for his dear sake.

As we remember
    the love of the cross,
we remember also
    the love of Bethlehem
and join with the angels
    in glory to thee
    and peace towards all.

Let my life, O God most high,
    be a daily gloria
    to Father, Son, and Holy Spirit.

Blessed be thou, O Lord God,
    in the highest
    and on earth,
    in time
    and in eternity,
    by saints and angels,
    by living and departed,
and by me,
    the object of thy love,
    the heir of thy grace,
    the partaker of thy life,
        today and always.

O Lord God,
  we know thy love
  in Jesus Christ whom thou
      didst send;
  we share his life.

Bless us with thy peace
  and keep us
      in thy love
        always.

# Acts of Thanksgiving

*1*
138

Grant, O most gracious Lord, that I may go in the
   strength of this food to be, and bear, and do all that
   is thy will for me.

Holy Spirit, remind me of thy strength within me and
   make me obedient and victorious in all that happens.

Lord Christ, grant that with thy life within me I may
   daily grow in thy likeness.

I am come to do thy will, O my God; I delight to do it
   for thy law is within my heart.

*2*
                                                    139

Lord,
now that I have partaken of thy life,
let me see other people through thine eyes,
let me have thy mind
in all the problems and decisions of life,
let the love of thy heart be in my heart,
let thy will strengthen my will,
let thy peace guard me in all alarm and anxiety,
and let thy presence go with me.

Lord Jesus, a last moment of gratitude,
for thy life, thy death and resurrection,
for this sacrament
of remembrance, love, and life,
and for the brethren
who have knelt with me at thine altar.

Lord, I can never love thee enough,
never thank thee enough:
Keep me thine for ever, today, tomorrow,
through this life,
and to all eternity,
O thou Giver of life, love, and blessing.

# The Divine Exercises

There is in Buddhism a lovely devotional practice in which the devout Buddhist sits in quiet meditation and radiates to all living beings love, joy, compassion, and peace in turn. The spirit of this practice is expressed in the Buddhist 'prayer' or aspiration:

> Now may every living thing, young or old, weak or strong, living near or far, known or unknown, living or departed or yet unborn, may every living thing be full of bliss.

The Thera-vada Buddhists in Burma, who were my friends, did not believe in an Eternal God, so the practice of these four good and noble exercises was a very humanistic one. Even at this humanistic level the exercise is a lovely thing which can be creative in the inner life and outlook of the man who uses it regularly. One day we shall know more of the solidarity of the human race and how waves of thought and feeling can move through our common or collective unconscious, and we may then learn of the effect of such radiation of love, joy, compassion, and peace in the minds and hearts of others.

I have tried to use these exercises in a framework of my belief in God-in-Christ, as daring to think of myself as a channel for his universal love or of adding my small contribution of love, joy, compassion, and peace to his infinitely more generous radiation.

O thou source of all love,
let thy love go out to all created beings,
to those I love and to those who love me,
to the few I know and to the many I do not know,
to all of every race,
to all the living in this world
and to all the living dead in the next world:
May all be free from evil and harm,
may all come to know thy love
and find the happiness
of loving thee and their fellows.
O let the small love of my heart
go out with thine all-embracing love
for the sake of him who first loved us
and taught us love,
even Jesus Christ, our Lord.

O thou, who art the joy of loving hearts,
let thy joy fill the hearts of all men everywhere—
the joy of knowing that the world is thy creation,
that men are called to be thy children,
that sin is forgiven,
that death has been conquered,
that thou art ever seeking men,
willing to live in them,
that thy will is righteousness, peace, and love.
Let this joy fill my heart,
the hearts of all my friends,

the hearts of all men everywhere;
let the whole universe be filled with thy joy,
through him who brought us joy,
even Jesus Christ, thy Son, our Lord.


## COMPASSION TO ALL                                    143

O thou Lord of all mercy,
let thy compassion go out
to all whom thou hast made,
to those who are sick or in pain,
to those who mourn,
to the lonely and to those without hope,
to all who sin and do not know
that thou thyself hast come to us in forgiveness,
to all who search for meaning
in the universe and in the life of man
and have not found the truth in thee.
Let thy mercy hold them, surround them,
penetrate them, save them,
so that they be thine for ever.
Increase in me thy mercy,
that my small compassion may accompany
thine infinite love,
in gratitude for thy mercy to me
and in love for those who through eternity
are to be my companions, sharers in the mercy
brought by thy Son, our Saviour and Redeemer.

May the peace which passes understanding
possess the minds of men everywhere,
banishing all anxiety and perplexity,
watching sentinel over their hearts and minds,
refusing entrance to every disturbing thought.
In everything that happens
may men know that all things work together for good
when they love thee and want thy will.
Give them thine own peace,
which the world cannot give and cannot take away.
Let nations live together in peace
and know the things that belong unto peace.
And may thy peace in my heart
go out to all my fellow men—
to calm their worries and their enmities,
to let them know that the peace given me
is available for them also,
through him who made himself men's Peace,
even Jesus Christ, our Lord.

# Hymn of Faith

All praise to thee, Eternal Lord,
Who on the primal chaos of the world didst brood
And looking aeons ahead in love's creative mood
    A universe didst see.
    Creator Lord, continue thy eternal plan.

The cell of life to matter's stuff
Was knit, and clothed the rock with herb and tree
As though preparing food for creatures yet to be,
    Pastures for flock and herd.
    Creator Lord, continue thy eternal plan.

Then in the waters life did stir
And in the slow unhurried passing of the years
Complexity, succeeding simpler forms, appears.
    Creatures of air and land
Set forward, Lord, another stage of thy eternal plan.

Upward and onward moving then,
The spreading tree of life fresh branches grew,
Some stayed content, declining progress new,
    Good in each kind complete
Yet not good enough for thy eternal plan.

The main stem still continued straight
Developing new form and brain and hand until,
As aeons passed, on earth a creature thou didst fill
    With spirit kin to thine,
And galaxies with angels hymned the birth of man.

Unfinished yet, this child of thine
Had yet to learn the secrets of his world and hour.
Seed life and harvest, fire, and atom's endless power
    Subdue and guide and use;
    No limit, Lord, to thy eternal plan.

The universe awaits the finished man,
The tree of life has still its final height to climb,
Unending years demand some focal point of time:
  This thou hast given, O Lord,
 In one short life, thyself hast said, 'Behold the man'.


 In him was life, the animating force,
Evolver of the universe, the power that moves the whole,
The light that lightens every man, in mind and heart and soul,
  Unrecognized before, yet speaking now,
 The Word that manifests the love in thy great plan.

 Can purpose ever cease? Ahead
Must lie new worlds of wonder, higher, fuller life,
A unity of God-like love, defeated death,
  So man with God shall look
 At their joint workmanship, and both declare it good.

 The eye of faith still peers ahead
Through human fog and dawn's receding gloom,
The final scene, no catastrophic fiery doom,
  But God's perfected plan
 When Christ shall offer back the universe and Man.

# Prayer after Praying

O God, having prayed these prayers,        146
I know that I do not have to implore
your mercy, love, and grace,
for you are more ready to give
than I to ask.
Rather, I need to pray
that I may be ready to receive your gifts,
humbly — eagerly — gratefully.
O Divine Spirit at work within men,
persuade us to do this,
so that we may hold
hands open and eager
to receive your bounty.

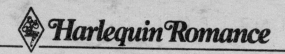
# Harlequin Romance

## Coming Next Month

Available in June wherever paperback books are sold, or through Harlequin Reader Service:

In the U.S.
901 Fuhrmann Blvd.
P.O. Box 1397
Buffalo, N.Y. 14240-1397

In Canada
P.O. Box 603
Fort Erie, Ontario
L2A 5X3

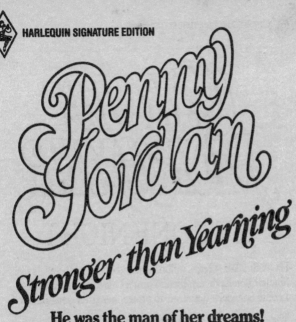

# Penny Jordan

## Stronger than Yearning

### He was the man of her dreams!

The same dark hair, the same mocking eyes; it was as if the Regency rake of the portrait, the seducer of Jenna's dream, had come to life. Jenna, believing the last of the Deverils dead, was determined to buy the great old Yorkshire Hall—to claim it for her daughter, Lucy, and put to rest some of the painful memories of Lucy's birth. She had no way of knowing that a direct descendant of the black sheep Deveril even existed—or that James Allingham and his own powerful yearnings would disrupt her plan entirely.

Penny Jordan's first Harlequin Signature Edition *Love's Choices* was an outstanding success. Penny Jordan has written more than 40 best-selling titles—more than 4 million copies sold.

Now, be sure to buy her latest bestseller, *Stronger Than Yearning*. Available wherever paperbacks are sold—in June.

# CAROLE MORTIMER

## JUST ONE NIGHT

Hawk Sinclair—Texas millionaire and owner of the exclusive
Sinclair hotels, determined to protect his son's inheritance.
Leonie Spencer—desperate to protect her sister's happiness.

They were together for just one night.
The night their daughter was conceived.

Blackmail, kidnapping and attempted murder add suspense
to passion in this exciting bestseller.

The success story of Carole Mortimer continues with *Just
One Night*, a captivating romance from the author of the
bestselling novels, *Gypsy* and *Merlyn's Magic*.

**Available in March
wherever paperbacks are sold.**

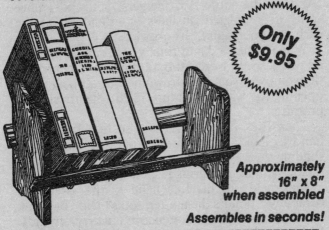

you down. I know you'll tell me, when you feel ready. As for me, I believe we two have a future together. I believe the Totem/*Doorsteps* merger will be our biggest success yet—take the market by storm.'

Before she could collect her wits to reply, he was pulling her to him again, with a rougher urgency. 'And on the subject of mergers, you and I have some uncompleted business to attend to, at the earliest opportunity,' he growled.

When Vanessa could finally speak, all she could do was echo: 'the earliest opportunity'. In her heart, the song was soaring, drowning out all past pain, opening the way to a future filled with music and promise.

Then Rick pushed the door so that they stood hand in hand, in the sudden pool of limelight—shading their eyes, smiling, translucent. All around them, sympathetic grins responded.

Rick held out his free hand to the assembled company. 'What's the matter, folks? Did you think we'd deserted you? You needn't worry, friends. We'll never be very far away—will, we, Vanessa?'

'No, Rick.' She beamed at everyone, especially Mark. 'Not far away.'